Residential Masterpieces 24

Mies van der Rohe
Villa Tugendhat
Brno, Czech, 1928-30

Text by Yoshio Futagawa

Photographed by Yukio Futagawa

世界現代住宅全集24
ミース・ファン・デル・ローエ
トゥーゲントハット邸
チェコ，ブルノ　1928-30

文・編集：二川由夫

企画・撮影：二川幸夫

求道的近代理念の拡張──二川由夫
Expansion of Essence-Seeking Principles *by Yoshio Futagawa*

20世紀近代建築のグル（指導者）の一人である巨匠ミース・ファン・デル・ローエは第二次大戦を境にその活躍の場をヨーロッパから新大陸アメリカに移すことになった。その移動は彼が建築界に問いかけるマニフェストを大きく変えることになる。その異なる二つのフェイズは結局20世紀建築を大きく動かして，次の世紀に建築を導いていく。

　ミースの戦前の仕事において最も重要な焦点となる実作の一つは1929年バルセロナ博のために建てられた通称「バルセロナ・パヴィリオン」(1928-29年)である。このパヴィリオンは会期の僅か半年の間だけ存在した幻のような建築であるにもかかわらず，その後の建築界に多大な影響を残すマスターピースであり，解体後半世紀を経て，復元され，現在その空間を体験することができるものである。「バルセロナ・パヴィリオン」で実現された未知の完全な建築，それは新しい空間制御の精微な理論であり，同時に建築のかつて持っていた厳格で正調な美学への回帰であった。平屋のパヴィリオンが示したのは新しい建築の試行──閉じない壁面の構成によってつくり出される哲学的で，かつ詩的な空間体験である。それは一つであるにもかかわらず緩やかに切断された複数の空間群であり，それらを移り行く新鮮な建築体験や，ある場所に滞在して他所から漂ってくる気配を「嗅ぐ」全体の建築の様

相，パヴィリオンは建物のフットプリントの領域を超え外部空間へ，そして世界と接続する画期的なものであった。また同時にパヴィリオンにより近代建築が伝統／歴史との再接続の可能性も示すことになる。近代建築の機能的な側面はそれまでの建築の担う装飾的な一面を否定し，離脱する態度から出発されたが，このパヴィリオンに展開する様々な美学的な仕掛けは抽象化されているもののそれ以前の伝統的／歴史的な美学の文脈に沿うものである。自然石の醸す優雅な紋様の壁，陽光や風といった自然の移ろいを映し出す水面，柔らかなカーテンによって様相を変えることができる空間，抽象化，近代化されたデザインであるにもかかわらず伝統的な文脈から逸脱しない家具──様々なテクスチャーや質感／重量感，それらが実現する空間のスケールやディテールの寸法の精微さ──ここに近代建築は，再び輝ける建築の歴史に確実に接続されていた。

　「バルセロナ・パヴィリオン」の設計とほぼ同時期に進行していた「トゥーゲントハット邸」(1928-30年)は，戦前ミースが実現した建築作品のピークとして並び称される二大傑作である。しかし，一方の「バルセロナ・パヴィリオン」が示した揺るぎのない究道的な姿──マニフェストとして明快な完結性を持つのに対して，「トゥーゲントハット邸」は同じ建築的理念を表明するも，全く

One of the gurus of the 20th-century modern architecture, the legendary architect Mies van der Rohe shifted his field of activity from Europe to the New World, America, since WWII. This move caused a significant change in his manifesto on various issues in the architecture industry. Eventually, the two different phases would affect the 20th-century architecture on a major scale and lead it toward the next century.

One of the most important focal point in Mies' pre-war completed projects is the Barcelona Pavilion (1928-29) built for the 1929 International Exposition in Barcelona. Despite the fact that this pavilion was like a phantom architecture that existed for half a year only for the length of the exposition, it is a masterpiece that left a significant influence on the architecture industry. Its reconstruction half a century after it was torn down allows people to visit and experience its space today. What was realized through Barcelona Pavilion was a perfect architecture of the unknown: a new, accurate theory on space control, as well as a return to the strict, orthodox aesthetics that architecture once had. The single-story pavilion was a demonstration of a new architectural experiment involving a philosophic yet poetic spatial experience created by a composition of walls that do not enclose. It offered fresh architectural experience of threading through clusters of spaces that are loosely disconnected all the while being integrated as one; the aspect of the entire architecture allowed visitors to 'take a sniff of' presences that float out from other areas. Cutting across

the building's footprint, the pavilion was revolutionary in that it tried to connect not only to the exterior space but also to the world beyond. At the same time, it demonstrated the possibility for the modern architecture to reconnect with tradition/history. Functional facets of modern architecture began with an attitude of rejecting the ornamental aspect with which architecture has been burdened with then breaking away from it. But the diverse aesthetic maneuvers that revolve around this pavilion are, although abstracted in form, in keeping with the earlier traditional/historical aesthetic context. Walls with elegant patterns derived from natural stone; water surface reflecting nature in transition such as sunlight and wind; spaces whose aspects can be adjusted by soft curtains; furniture that do not deviate from traditional context despite its abstract, modern design; accuracy of size in the details as well as scale of space realized by various textures, surface characters and senses of weight—everything accounted for a reliable reconnection between modern architecture and the glorious history of architecture.

Designed around the same time, Barcelona Pavilion and Villa Tugendhat (1928-30) are two masterpieces that are ranked at the peak among the architectural works that Mies completed before WWII. While Barcelona Pavilion has a clear completeness as a manifesto, shown as an unshakable essence-seeking attitude, Villa Tugendhat is, although indicative of the same architectural principles, a residential architecture as a particu-

異なる方向性／可能性を同時に示す住宅建築としての特殊解であり，傑作である。

　1928年，ミースはコレクターで歴史家のエドゥアルド・フックスに依頼されたベルリンにある住宅の増築を完成させた。以前よりこの住宅に出入りしていた女性，グレーテ・ウェイス（ウェイスは最初の夫の名字，旧姓はロウ＝ビア）は，故郷チェコ，ブルノにフリッツ・トゥーゲントハットとの結婚を機に新居を建てることとなり，フックスに建築家のミースを紹介された。グレーテはフックス邸でのミースの仕事や「ヴァイセンホーフ・ジートルンク」(1927年)にたいへん好感を持っており，即座にミースに新居を設計を依頼することになった。新居は夫人の父親からの結婚祝いであり，敷地はブルノの街から北に向かって登る丘の中腹，夫人の両親宅の敷地の一部であった。その敷地は北側上端をシュバルツフェルド通りに面し，そこから南側にある両親宅に向かってなだらかに下っていく広大な斜面で，通りのレベルからブルノの街のシンボルであるシュビルベルク古城が正面に見える素晴らしい場所である。ミースはこの眺望を最大限に生かし，夫人の父親からの潤沢な資金提供の元，20世紀において最も贅を尽くした近代住宅の一つである名作住宅建築を完成させた。

住宅は基本的に三つのレベルを持つ。寝室群の置かれた通りに面した上階，居間と食堂のある主階，さらに下にある基壇部分にあたる機械室や倉庫などの様々なサービス機能を収めたレベルからなる。

　北側のシュバルツフェルド通りから見るこの住宅は1層の開口部の少ない水平方向に伸びた白く無口で控えめな存在である。寝室群が収まる東側のヴォリュームと車庫や使用人のための諸室をおさめる西側のヴォリュームは1枚の屋根スラブで結ばれ，その間に玄関ホールと階段室の収まる乳白色のガラス壁と，南側の寝室のためのテラスに至る開口部が与えられた玄関テラスが配置される。その開口部は，街とシュビルベルク城の風景を小さく切り取っている。訪問者は階段室の半円形のガラス壁と1本の柱によって玄関に迎えられる。

　玄関ホールは乳白色のガラス壁がもたらす明るく柔らかい光が満ちている。このシンプルな空間はトラバーチンの床と1本の輝くクローム柱によって特別な場所となっている。玄関ホールの背後には東西にずらされて配置された二対の寝室――夫妻の二つの寝室と，子供たちの二つの寝室が置かれる。子供たちの寝室の前には遊び場のパティオが設けられた。子供たちの寝室の背後にはナニーのための部屋がある。

lar solution and a masterpiece that shows totally different directions/possibilities simultaneously.

In 1928, Mies finished an extension project for a house in Berlin commissioned by the art collector and historian Eduard Fuchs. When a woman who had been frequenting this house named Grete Weiss (Weiss being her first husband's last name, her maiden name was Löw-Beer) decided to build a new home in her hometown Brno, Czechoslovakia on her marriage to Fritz Tugendhat, Fuchs introduced her to an architect: Mies. Grete, having been impressed with Mies' work such as Fuchs' home and Weissenhof Estate (1927), immediately asked Mies to design her new home. A wedding present from Grete's father, the site of the new home was located halfway up a hill north of Brno, on the premises of Grete's parents' house. Bordered by Schwarzfeld street on its north end, the site is an expansive slope descending southward to the parents' house: a magnificent location with a street-level front view of the old Spilberk Castle, a landmark of the city of Brno. Making the most of this view, Mies brought to completion a masterpiece of residential architecture, one of the most luxurious modern residence of the 20th century, amply funded by Grete's father.

The home consists basically of three levels: upper level facing the street where the bedrooms are located; main level housing the living and dining rooms; and the lower, platform level accommodating various service functions such as machine room and storage.

Viewed from the Schwarzfeld street on the north, the house is a white, reticent and demure presence, single-layered, with few apertures and stretching along the horizontal direction. The volume on the east with the bedrooms and the volume on the west with the garage and various rooms for the servants are connected via a sheet of roof slab. Arranged in between are the milk-white glass wall housing the entrance hall and staircase, and a entrance terrace with aperture leading to the bedroom on the south. This aperture frames a small view of the city and the Spilberk Castle. At the entrance, visitors are greeted by the semi-circular glass wall of the staircase and a column.

Bright soft light from the milk-white glass wall fills the entrance hall; this simple space is turned into a special place by installing a travertine floor and a shiny chrome column. Behind the entrance hall are two pairs of bedrooms arranged separately on east and west: two bedrooms for the couple and another two for the children. In front of the children's bedrooms is a patio serving as a play area. Behind the children's bedrooms is their nanny's room.

Stepping down the stairs in the entrance hall, the 180-degree turn around the chrome column leads to the glazed door to the main level. The latter is a vast open-plan space comprising the living and dining rooms and study/library, with service rooms to back them up from behind arranged on the west. Nestled between a seamless white linoleum floor and a

玄関ホールの階段をクロームの柱を180度回るように降りていくと，主階へのガラス扉に至る。主階は居間，食堂，書斎／図書室からなる一室の大空間であり，それをバックアップするサービスのための諸室が西側背後に配置されている。大空間は白いリノリウムのシームレスな床と漆喰の白い天井に挟まれ，居間，食堂，書斎／図書室の諸空間群は縞瑪瑙（めのう）の平面壁と黒檀の半円形の壁の2枚の壁によって閉じることなく緩やかに区別される。

これら明快に材料と形状の異なる2枚の壁は，主構造であるクロームに被覆された十字柱が5メートル間隔で整然と行進する一室の大空間を緩やかに仕切る。伝統的な住宅にある諸室の機能や関係性を近代的に翻訳し，さらに，ミースのデザインした様々な家具群が壁の規定する様々な場に置かれることで，近代的に新しくも伝統と乖離することのない，豊かな日常生活を実現していた。美しい紋様の縞瑪瑙の壁は居間と書斎／図書室を分け，一方半円形の壁はその中心に丸テーブルを持つ食堂を囲む求心的な空間をつくり出している。食堂やその他の諸用途の空間は天井のレールを沿うカーテンによってそれぞれ完全に閉じることもできる。

主階の大空間は鉄骨造の恩恵によってその外縁に構造エレメントを持たないため，東，南面は天井高一杯のガラス壁が与えられる。東側は温室を挟んだ2枚のガラス壁であり，南側は広大な庭と街や城のパノラマ風景を見渡すガラス壁である。東側温室の植物は外の庭の風景とオーバーラップされ，厚みのある緑の壁を室内へ視覚的に提供する。南側は長手方向に五つに分割されたガラス壁であり，そのうちの2枚の窓は電動で床の下に降ろすことができ，内外は完全に一体化される。南側ガラス壁の上部には可動式の日除けが収納され，夏の陽光を遮ることもできる。食堂の西側，トラバーチン貼りの屋外テラスが庭に突き出すように配置されている。居間／食堂とテラスはガラス壁や開閉式の大窓を介して視覚的，空間的に結ばれ，それぞれに起きている出来事を直接的に認識させる。テラスから同じトラバーチンによる大階段が建物の長手方向に沿って庭に降りていく。

庭は緩やかに南に向かって下っていく斜面であり，前述の階段から伸びる小径は豊かな緑の庭をまっすぐ下っていき，敷地の東端に沿って再び登り，温室にある建物入口に至るループを形づくっている。庭から見上げる住宅は3層のモダン・ヴィラであり，シュバルツフェルド通りの控えめなファサードとは全く違うスケール感を持ち，開放的なファサードである。それはギリシャの神殿やパラディオのヴィラなどが放つ建築の雄弁な姿と同義的な美学に基づいている。

white plaster ceiling, the cluster of spaces—living room, dining room, study/library—is mildly separated yet never enclosed by two walls: a flat wall in onyx and a semi-circular wall in Macassar ebony.

Clearly different in material and shape, these two walls mildly partition the vast open-plan space marked by an orderly procession of chrome-clad cruciform-shaped columns standing at 5-meter intervals. A modern interpretation of functions and relationships of various rooms found in a traditional house combined with various pieces of furniture designed by Mies arranged in various places defined by the walls contribute to the realization of a rich daily life that is modern and new but do not lose touch with tradition. Beautifully patterned wall of onyx separates the living room from the study/library, while the semi-circular wall creates a centripetal space around a dining room with a round table in the center. The dining room and other functional areas can be completely closed with curtains that run along the rails attached to the ceiling.

Since the vast space on the main level do not have any structural elements along its outer edges thanks to its steel frame structure, the east and south facades each feature a full-height glass wall: the former is a double glass wall housing a winter garden in between; the latter offers a panoramic view over the expansive garden, the cityscape beyond and the castle. Plants in the eastern winter garden overlap with the exterior landscape of the garden, visually introducing a thick wall of green to the interior. The southern glass wall is divided longitudinally into five segments, with two of them being power-retractable in a pocket under the floor to completely integrate the indoors with the outdoors. Stored above the southern glass wall is a retractable awning that blocks sunlight during summer. On the western side of the dining room is an outdoor terrace clad in travertine that protrudes into the garden. Glass walls and large retractable window panes connect the living and dining rooms with the terrace both visually and spatially, making it possible for activities in both areas to be directly acknowledged reciprocally. From the terrace, a grand staircase of the same travertine climbs down to the garden along the building's longitudinal side.

The garden is a slope that gradually descends to the south. A path stretches out from the aforementioned stairs, makes a descent straight across the garden, climbs up along the site's eastern border and reaches an entrance to the building in the winter garden, forming a loop. Looking up from the garden, the house is a three-story modernist villa with an open facade in a scale that is totally different from other facades found on Schwarzfeld street, one which is based on the aesthetics synonymous with those eloquent images that emanate from architectures such as Greek temples and Palladian villas.

The lower level in the platform houses various service functions such as a huge repository for garden furniture, laundry room, storage, and darkroom for the husband who was a photo

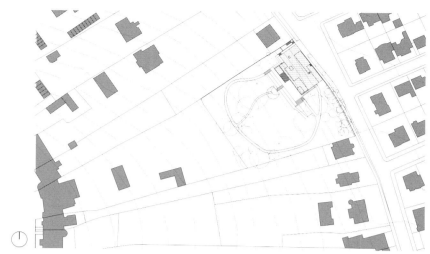

Site plan S=1:3000

　基壇となる下階はサービス機能を納める。庭の家具などのための巨大な倉庫，洗濯室や貯蔵庫，そして主人の趣味であった写真のための暗室などが配置される。さらに，機械室の数々，当時としては異例に先進的であった冷暖房のシステム，前述の機械式のガラス窓の昇降メカニズムといった，近代建築が当時の先進技術を積極的に取り入れて機能的なパフォーマンスを演じる，その役割に対するバックアップ・スペースとなっている。

「トゥーゲントハット邸」もまた，「バルセロナ・パヴィリオン」の短命な末路と同様の悲劇的な運命を辿っている。完成後10年も経たない1938年，ナチス・ドイツのチェコ進攻の前年にユダヤ人のトゥーゲントハット一家は亡命し，その後この名作建築は長い間様々な用途に供され，改築され，破壊され，建築史の確固たる1ページを飾るものであるにもかかわらず，幻となってしまう。

　1986年，ミース・ファン・デル・ローエ100回目の誕生日を機に「バルセロナ・パヴィリオン」が50年以上の歳月を経て再建されるが，同じ頃より「トゥーゲントハット邸」も時代の翻弄から解き放されることとなる。建物は世紀末に向けて時間をかけて徐々に修復され，家具や設えは忠実に再現され，今日，再び竣工当時の輝きを取り戻している。

　公開される二つの傑作を実際に体験することで，ミースが如何に当時，近代建築の理念と可能性を実現し，同時に過去の価値観と繋げて歴史の道筋を通し，次の時代を目指していたかを知ることとなろう。そして，如何にバルセロナとブルノの二つの記念碑的名作がミースの異なる建築への態度であったかを物語っている。先鋭化，研ぎ澄まされていく完全な理念と，反対に広く浸透，拡散しうる柔軟な可能性——フィクショナルな揺るぎない普遍的な精神的／哲学的な理念と，リアルな日常世界に沿う高次元な機能的秩序／合理的システムが，高い品格を保ちながらも日常の様々な流動のバリエーションを許容して，さらに世界，大衆に拡散し得る可能性である。

「トゥーゲントハット邸」に示された建築的な戦略は，高次な理念が如何にクライアントを持ち得て要求されたプログラムに柔軟に対応し，日常の変化に対抗して常に輝き続けるかということへの試行であった。クライアントは大変裕福な一家であり，高いクオリティの日常生活の舞台としての住宅はさまざまな要望を許容して実現された。その再現不可能なほどの贅沢を纏った住宅は近代建築理念の結晶であるとともに彼らの華麗な暮らしを機能させるものであり，さらにこのマニフェストには矛盾するような，一般的な価値観にまで拡散し得る可能性すら示されていたのである。

enthusiast. In addition, there are spaces and machine rooms to back up the roles of a modern architecture that performed state-of-the-art functions of the time such as the astonishingly cutting-edge air-conditioning system and the elevator mechanism for the aforementioned retractable glass windows.

Villa Tugendhat eventually followed the same tragic fate as the short-lived Barcelona Pavilion. In 1938, less than 10 years after its completion, the Jewish family of the Tugendhats having fled the country a year prior to the German Nazi invasion of Czechoslovakia, this architectural masterpiece worthy of a full-page entry in the history of architecture was seized and put to various uses for a long time; it was remodeled, damaged and ultimately reduced to an illusion.

　In 1986, on the occasion of the 100th anniversary of Mies van der Rohe's birth, Barcelona Pavilion came to be reconstructed more than 50 years after its demolition. It was around the same time that Villa Tugendhat also managed to set itself free from the mercy of the times. Its building was gradually restored over time from one century to another; furniture and fittings were reproduced authentically. Today, it regained its original luster from the time of completion.

　Through an on-site experience of the two masterpieces that are now open to public, we are able to learn how Mies worked toward the next era, materializing theories and possibilities of modern architecture of the time and at the same time connecting them with values from the past to pave the way of history. The two monumental works in Barcelona and Brno both represent Mies' different attitudes toward architecture: sharp, heightened principles of the perfect versus flexible potentials that are likely to pervade and diffuse; fictional, unshakable spiritual/philosophical principles versus high-level functional order or rational system that keep with the real world of daily life—that are found in his pursuit of an architecture that would tolerate fluid variations of daily life while maintaining dignity and grace, with a potential of diffusing into the public as well as into the world.

　His architectural strategy demonstrated in Villa Tugendhat was an attempt over the issue of how a high order of principles would be able to engage clients, respond flexibly to required programs, play against daily changes and continue to shine evermore. In this case the client was a notably wealthy family, and their home as a stage for a high-quality daily life was realized by tolerating all sorts of requests. Clad in luxury that is almost impossible to duplicate, the house is not only a crystallization of modern architectural principles but is also what makes the family's upscale living function. What is more, this manifesto indicated a contradictory potential of diffusing itself even into general values.

English translation by Lisa Tani

View from garden toward Spilberk Castle on hill afar

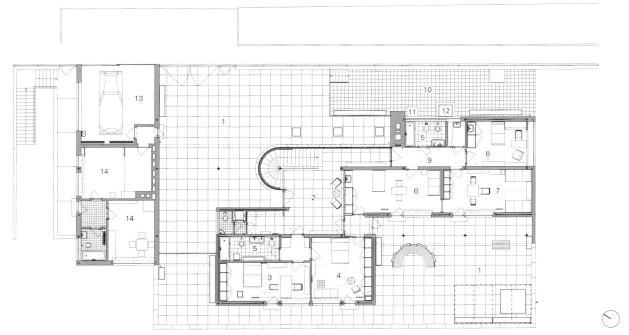

Third floor (street level) S=1:300

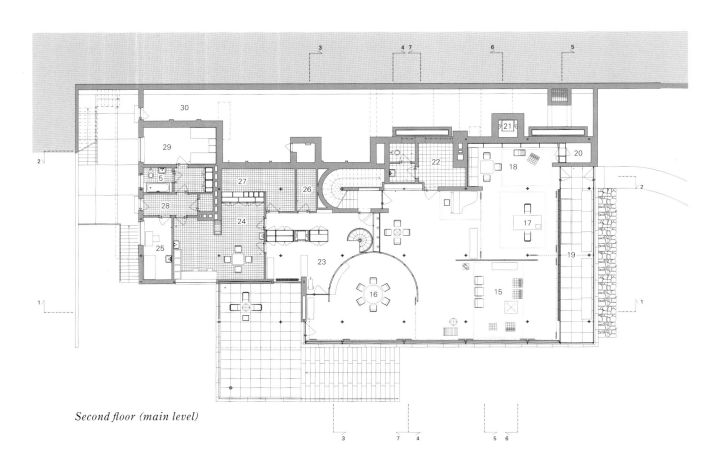

Second floor (main level)

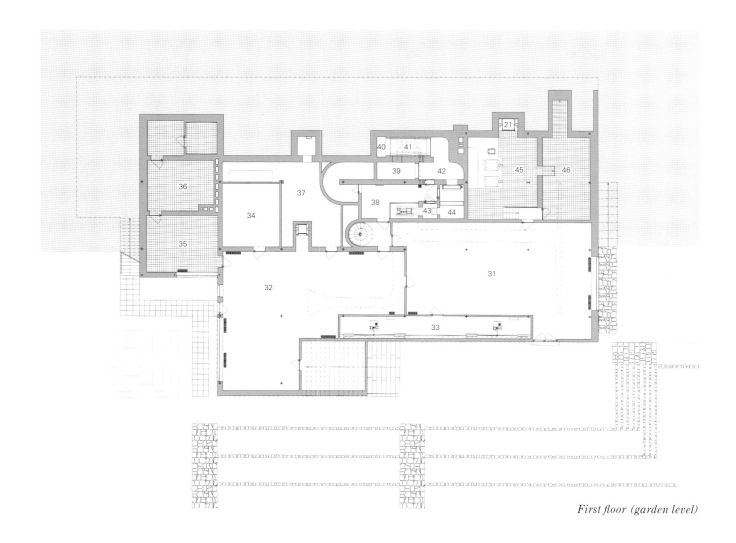

First floor (garden level)

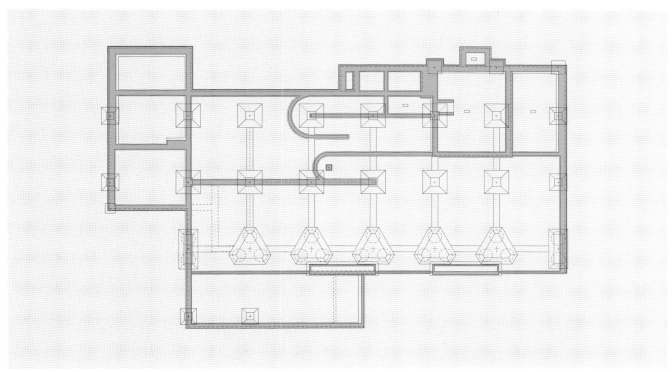

Foundation and pilotis

1 TERRACE	14 CARETAKER'S ROOM	27 PANTRY	36 DARK ROOM
2 ENTRANCE HALL	15 LIVING ROOM	28 REAR ENTRANCE	37 STOREROOM WITH RESERVE RAINWATER
3 FRITZ'S BEDROOM	16 DINING ROOM	29 SERVANT'S ROOM	38 MECHANICAL ROOM FOR AIR TECHNOLOGY
4 GRETE'S BEDROOM	17 STUDY	30 AIR INSULATION CAVITY	
5 BATHROOM	18 LIBRARY	31 STOREROOM FOR GARDEN FURNITURE	39 OUTTAKE FOR USED AIR
6 CHILDREN'S ROOM (BOYS)	19 CONSERVATORY		40 INTAKE FOR FRESH AIR
7 CHILDREN'S ROOM (GIRLS)	20 ROOM FOR SAFE	32 DRYING ROOM FOR LAUNDRY AND IRONING	41 COOLING AND DRYING AIR
8 NANNY'S ROOM	21 ASH LIFT		42 MIXING CHAMBER
9 CORRIDOR	22 PROJECTION ROOM	33 MECHANICAL ROOM FOR RETRACTING WINDOWS	43 HEATING AIR
10 TECHNICAL TERRACE	23 PREPARATION ROOM FOR FOOD		44 AIR FILTER
11 OUTTAKE DUCT	24 KITCHEN	34 STOREROOM FOR FRUITS AND VEGETABLES	45 BOILER ROOM
12 ASH LIFT COVER	25 COOK'S ROOM		46 COAL ROOM WITH COAL CHUTE
13 GARAGE	26 STORAGE	35 LAUNDRY ROOM	

House sits on top of sloped site

Mies van der Rohe

Villa Tugendhat

Residential Masterpieces 24
Mies van der Rohe
Villa Tugendhat

Text and edited by Yoshio Futagawa
Photographed by Yukio Futagawa
Art direction: Gan Hosoya

Copyright © 2016 A.D.A. EDITA Tokyo Co., Ltd.
3-12-14 Sendagaya, Shibuya-ku, Tokyo 151-0051, Japan
All rights reserved. No part of this publication may be reproduced,
stored in a retrieval system, or transmitted,
in any form or by any means, electronic, mechanical,
photocopying, recording, or otherwise,
without permission in writing from the publisher.

Copyright of photographs
©2016 GA photographers

Printed and bound in Japan

ISBN 978-4-87140-649-9 C1352

Overall view from garden on southwest

View from garden through willow

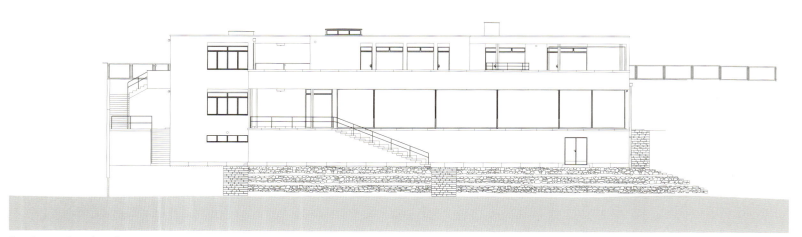
Southwest elevation S=1:300

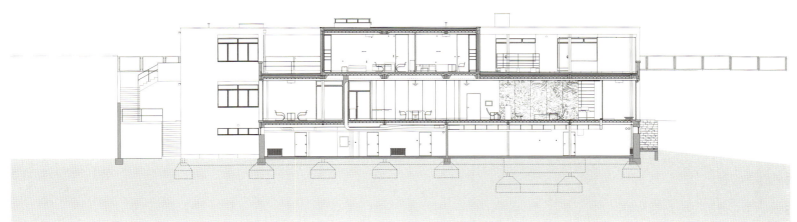

Section 1 S=1:300

View from west, before restoration finished in 2012 (1994)

Northeast view from street

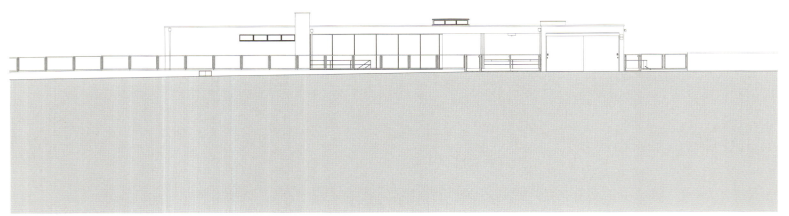

Northeast elevation S=1:300

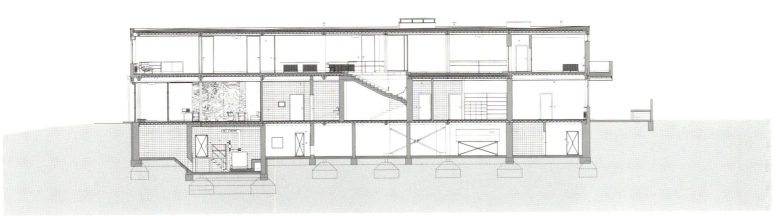

Section 2 S=1:300

23

Entrance terrace

Entrance terrace: looking toward street

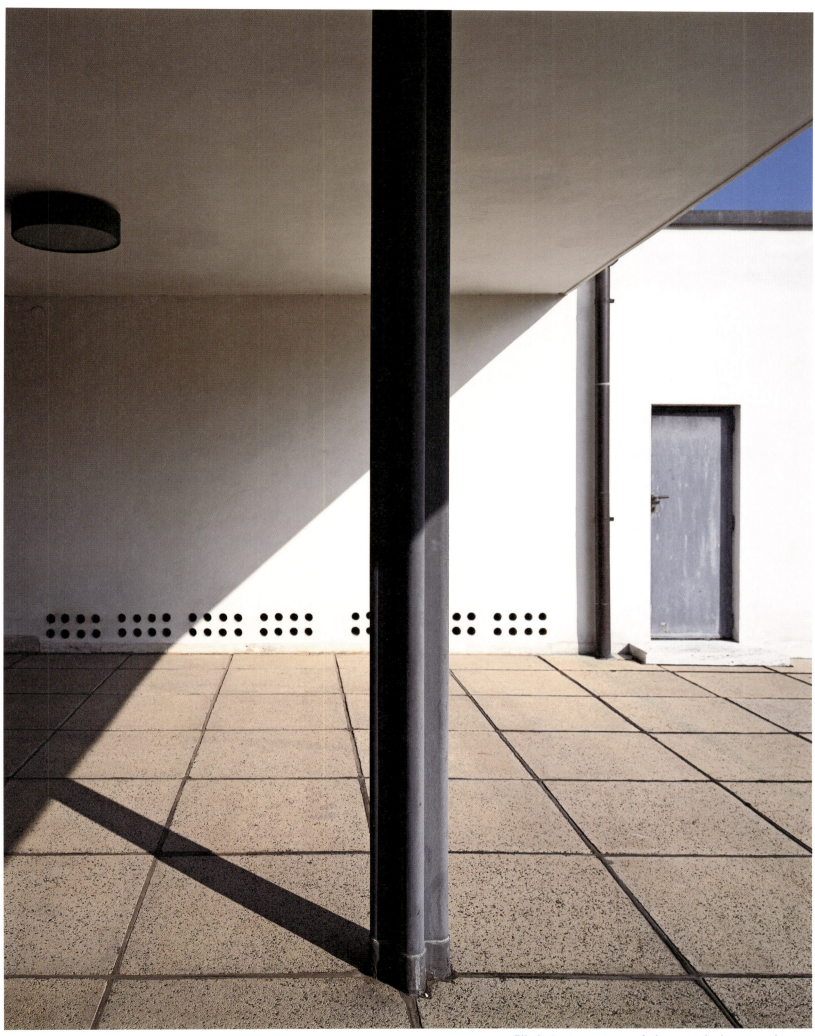

Piloti at entrance terrace facing caretaker's room and garage

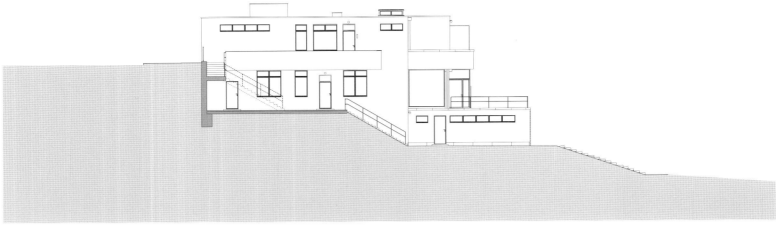
Northwest elevation S=1:300

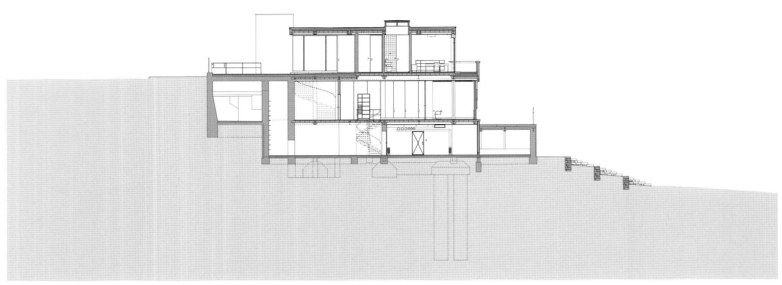
Section 3 S=1:300

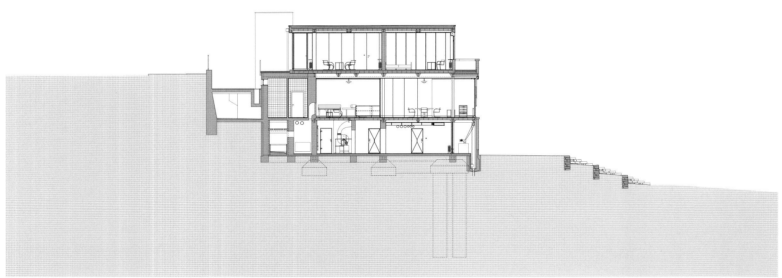
Section 4

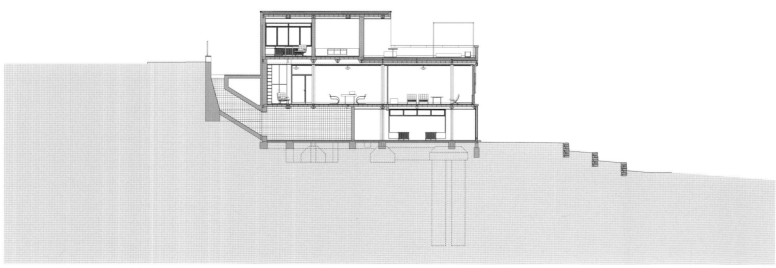
Section 5

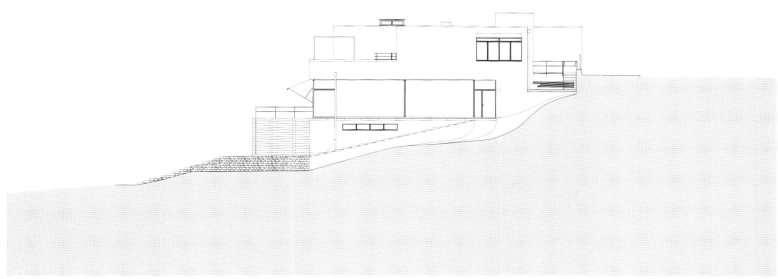

Southeast elevation S=1:300

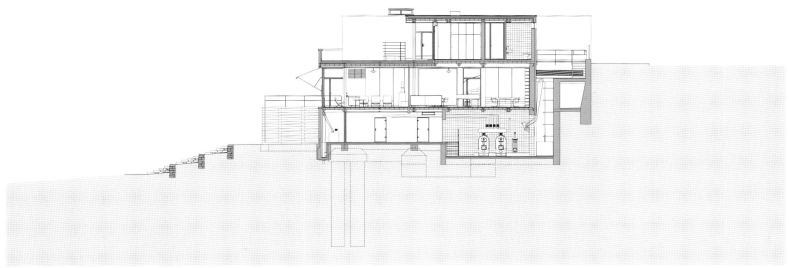

Section 6

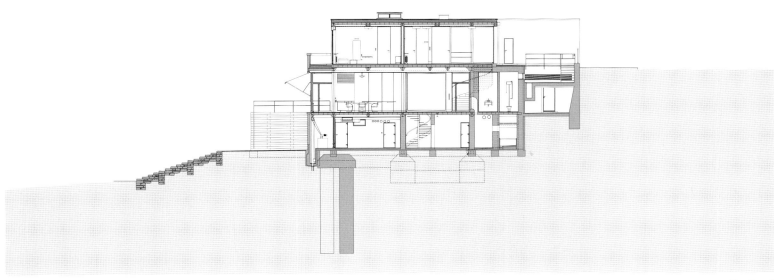

Section 7

Entrance terrace

Technical terrace lower than entrance level

Piloti and entrance

Entrance on third floor (street level)

Entrance hall. Staircase to main level below

Entrance hall

Staircase to main level below

Steel column at staircase

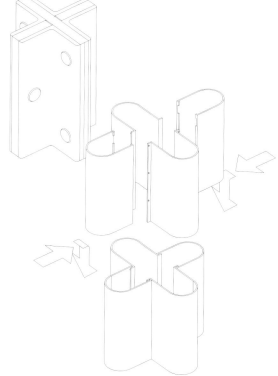

Axonometric of steel column

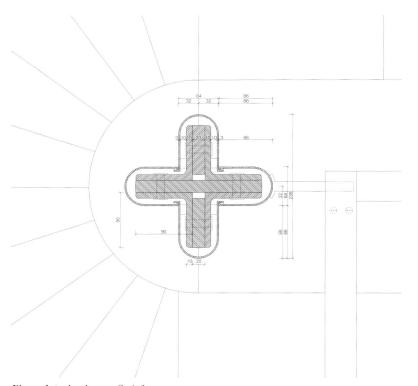

Plan of steel column S=1:6

Staircase

View from staircase. Entrance hall on right, children's bedrooms inmost

View from entry of living room on second floor

View toward entry of living room (there was no furniture in 1994)

40

View from entry of living room toward conservatory

Living room: view toward conservatory

Living room: view toward dining room

Living room: view toward garden and Spilberk Castle afar

Living room: onyx wall, Macassar ebony wall and steel column

48

Perimeter of living room: large windows are retractable to below

Study facing conservatory

Conservatory

Conservatory: view from study

Garden on southeast. Conservatory on right

Staircase from garden to living room on southwest

Terrace of living room

Dining room on right, terrace and staircase on left

Detail of retracting window

Detail of gap for retracting window

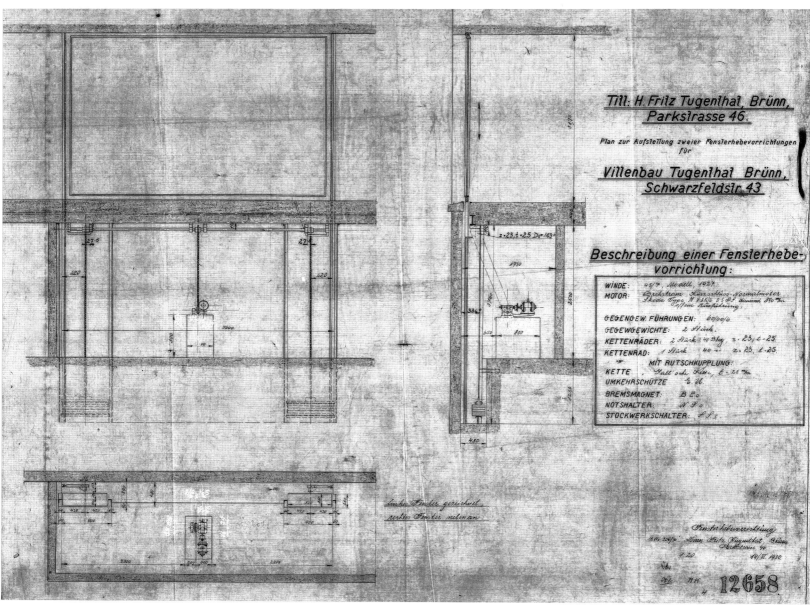

Drawing of retracting window

Dining room with circular table and semi-circular Macassar ebony wall

Study and library

Library

60

Entry of living room

Fritz Tugendhat's bedroom

Grete Tugendhat's bedroom

Master bathroom

Grete Tugendhat's bedroom

Terrace of bedrooms

Children's room (girls)

Children's room (boys)

View toward terrace from children's room (girls)

Steel column at terrace front of children's room (girls)

Partial southwest elevation: caretaker's room, kitchen and laundry room inside

Northwest porch: rear entrance on left

Preparation room for food. Dining room on right

Kitchen: looking garden

Kitchen

Storeroom for garden furniture on first floor (now exhibition gallery)

Steel column without cladding on first floor

Laundry room

*Mechanical room for air technology.
Air conditioning (heating and cooling) control panel on center*

Mechanical room for retracting windows

Mixing chamber

*Heating or cooling air from mixing chamber goes through
fliters (left and right) to rooms inside*

Photographs are taken by Yukio Futagawa in 1994 except as noted below.
pp.10-11, pp.14-15, pp.18-19, pp.30-31, pp.34-36, pp.38-39, p.41, p.44-47, pp.50-64, p.66, p.67 below, pp.70-71: photos by Yoshio Futagawa, taken in 2016
Drawing of p.58: courtesy of Brno City Museum
Drawings as follows: new drawings © Ivan Wahla, 2016
p.9 (site plan)
pp.12-13 (4 plans)
pp.18-19 (southwest elevation, section 1)
pp.22-23 (northeast elevation, section 2)
pp.28-29 (northwest elevation, section 3-7, southeast elevation)
p.36 (plan and axonometric of steel column at staircase)

世界現代住宅全集 24
ミース・ファン・デル・ローエ
トゥーゲントハット邸
2016 年 11 月 25 日発行
文・編集：二川由夫
撮影：二川幸夫
アート・ディレクション：細谷巌

印刷・製本：大日本印刷株式会社
制作・発行：エーディーエー・エディタ・トーキョー
151-0051　東京都渋谷区千駄ヶ谷 3-12-14
TEL. (03) 3403-1581 (代)

禁無断転載

ISBN 978-4-87140-649-9 C1352